The Laws of Falling Bodies

The Nicholas Roerich Poetry Prize

is an annual first-book competition sponsored by the
Nicholas Roerich Museum in New York City

1988
The Volcano Inside by David Dooley

1989
Without Asking by Jane Ransom

1990
Death, But at a Good Price by Chris Semansky

1991 co-winners
The Buried Houses by David Mason
Desire's Door by Lee McCarthy

1992
30 Miles from J-Town by Amy Uyematsu

1993
House Without a Dreamer by Andrea Hollander Budy

1994
Counterpoint by David Alpaugh

1995
The Silent Partner by Greg Williamson

1996
Infidelities by Elise Paschen

1997 co-winners
January Rain by Daniel Anderson
The Laws of Falling Bodies by Kate Light

Each volume of the Nicholas Roerich Poetry Prize Library is in
print and available from:
Story Line Press, Three Oaks Farm, Brownsville, OR 97327

The Laws of Falling Bodies

Kate Light

Story Line Press
1997

Published by Story Line Press, Inc., Three Oaks Farm, P.O. Box 1108, Ashland, OR 97520-0052

This publication was made possible thanks in part to the generous support of the Nicholas Roerich Museum, the Andrew W. Mellon Foundation, the Charles Schwab Corporation Foundation and our individual contributors.

Cover credit: Bruno Jarret, black & white photograph of Rodin's "La Danaide"

Cover design by Chiquita Babb

Text design by M. Rae Thompson

Library of Congress Cataloging-in-Publication Data

Light, Kate
    The laws of falling bodies
       p. cm.
    ISBN 1-885266-55-3
    1. Love poetry. I. Title.
    PS3562.I45392L38 1997
    811'.54--dc21   97-27243
                                  CIP

Acknowledgments

The author gratefully acknowledges the editors of the following publications in which these poems originally appeared:

Blue Unicorn: "Oh It Is All The Work Of Getting There"
Confrontation: "Under Simplicity"
The Christian Science Monitor: "And Then There Is That Incredible Moment"
Edge City Review: "Mass," and "Want and Love"
Feminist Studies: "The Idea Of Love Between Us"
Hellas: "Mostly"
Janus: "Daybook," "Reading Someone Else's Love Poems," and "Lines Written While Reading Keats' *Isabella; or, the Pot of Basil*"
The Paris Review: "Central Park" (as "Can One Think"), "San Francisco," "Portrait Of David As/Not As Refrigerator Magnet: Universal," "Another Urban Love Song: *Souvenir de Florence*...David Continues On His Way," and "Help Me" (as "Five Urban Love Songs")
Pivot: "You know how it is..." and "The Tender Gesture Can Resurrect The World"
Sparrow: "Home," "The Problem," and "Rules Of The Game" from "The Death of Albrecht"
Western Humanities Review: "After The Season," "Martha," "Erick And Martha," "The Weeks," and "About Sonnets Of Love; Some"
Wisconsin Review: "The Laws Of Falling Bodies"

—with love and gratitude to my family; and to Nicole Federici, Ann Rower, David Israel, Johanna Keller, Suzanne Noguere, Reinmar Seidler, Lois Finkel, Michael Milburn, Sylvia Kahan, Bruce Dunlap, Jerome Kitzke, Hilary Brown, and Alexa Wing; special thanks to Robert McDowell at Story Line Press; to the Erick Hawkins Dance Foundation; to Molly Peacock, Richard Howard, Dana Gioia, Agha Shahid Ali, and Grace Schulman; and Greg Hesselink, without whom....

CONTENTS

The Dance

The New Friend

At Sea

Want And Love

Coda

The Dance

Reading Someone Else's Love Poems

is, after all, all we've ever done
for centuries — except write them — but what
a strange thing it is, after all, rose-cheeks and sun-
hair and lips, and underarms, and that little gut
I love to nuzzle on, soft underbelly — oops —
that wasn't what I meant to talk about;
ever since handkerchiefs fell, and hoop-
skirts around ankles swirled
and smiled, lovers have dreamed their loves upon
the pages, courted and schemed and twirled
and styled, hoping that once they'd unfurled their down-
deep longing, they would have their prize —
not the songs of love, but love beneath disguise.

About Sonnets Of Love; Some

complain of us frozen there, a pile
of praised body parts, objectified;
bundle of hair and heart and breast and smile;
killed off line by line, petrified.
I think it's true the dying of the moments
begins in their capture —and maybe a man who's
unable to face his own aging laments
the woman's, saying *so fades the rose*,
and like that. Still I sympathize;
I struggle too with how to praise —
and yet do not want to advertise —
or exploit —my lover's secret lovely gaze.
Oh elegant beautiful spilling from the cup
of love my love how I could drink you up

The Weeks

A week alone than with your lover passes
differently. The week alone is perky and diverse,
the week the lover shares — wistful, slow, molasses.
I am not saying one is better or one worse —
only the *quality* is different. Underlying
the shared week, sadness counterpoints the dance —
(as if to leave would be no less than dying)
but alone again, the days go whizzing, flying
and are gone. So each is lived, as if a trance
cannot be broken, a promise must be kept.
And in each lies nostalgia for the other.
Then all along in each the other slept!
To keep the one and not to have the other...
you could not — except by trauma or by force.
Once broken, would you heal, or feel with terrible remorse
that weeks are years, and dry up at their source?

Broad Daylight

"...If it wasn't for broad daylight, and cooking stoves, and roosters, I'm afraid you would have occasion to smile at my letters often, but so sure as this mortal essays immortality, a crow from a neighboring farmyard dissipates the illusion, and I am here again."
Emily Dickinson, *letter*

Broad daylight, and cooking stoves, and ringing phones,
tiles shaken loose, and towels hanging at odd angles,
and paper bags, and measuring cups, and mail that fell
in, in tangles;
piles of pennies and matches and hairclips, and paperclips,
masking tape and clear tape and tape for wrapping cuts
incurred on dance floors, rows of recordings and books
and scores
and sounds of sirens, and glass breaking in the streets,
rehearsals beginning and ending with footsteps on the
stairs —
if it wasn't for these...
glass bowls, newspapers on doorsteps with
their magazines gloss-eager to be consumed —
all these would have to be exhumed —
and then perhaps — freed like arms pressed up against
the wall, then
released — I would float, simple as that! no more waiting,
no more weight at my throat! and my back — just like *that* —
would unbend;
and I'd fly right to you, and be there again, my friend!

Home

As in two brothers, one dark, one light,
one slow, one quick, both parents are yet inherent,
so my love and I of both separation and delight —
those feuding siblings — are the parents.
As two sisters, though opposed, bear the family
resemblance — so, in closeness and far-
off, my love and I (their tenders) are
still found. There is that homily
about home — its sweetness — and so do I say
wherever he is, it is homelike to me — sweet —
someplace I imagine I could stay —
a maxim I could repeat and repeat —
if only I were not so light on my feet —
and so quick, my brothers, to run away.

Mass

We lean on trees and stone buildings.
Solid structures reassure us
because our tiny bodies can be crushed.
(How? Like birds.) We pose stubbornly,
make much of ourselves, though we are fragile
at our cores. We gesture
toward each other, hiding our weakness, and that we are shaken
up — at dawn, at sunset, singing giddily
in a display of certainty and boldness.
We lean on trees and strong buildings,
though we can live on music, which is made of air.
Today we breakfasted on a Mass, many-winged,
hungry for company.

Hungry for company,
today we breakfasted *en masse*, many-winged…
Though we can live on music, which is made of air,
we lean on trees and strong buildings.
In a display of certainty and boldness,
up at dawn, at sunset, singing giddily
toward each other — hiding our weakness, and that we are shaken
at our cores — we gesture,
make much of ourselves. Though we are fragile
(how *like* birds), we pose stubbornly.
Because our tiny bodies can be crushed,
solid structures reassure us.
We lean on trees and stone buildings,

mass.

Your Unconscious Speaks To My Unconscious

Your unconscious speaks to my unconscious
like subtitles of another language, saying:
Why? Why did you do this
to me? So while we are laughing and playing,
my unconscious, hearing, says, *What did I*
do? Now yours is crying, weeping, saying,
Why are you doing this? Why
do you leave me? Aren't you staying?
And mine, astonished, says, *Sweetheart, I*
am right here. I am here. Your eyes
looking into mine. Your fingers in my hair.
But as our spines bend, something unties
in me, and I *am* no longer there.
For I have already watched you go,
in the movie, in the darkness, through the snow.

Under Simplicity

lies complexity. Under a word
lies the life that led, or was led,
up to the saying. Under what you said
were all the years I never heard,
all the questions unasked, or unanswered;
and the tones of voice that rose and fell, lead-
en in your consciousness. To me you said,
when I said certain things, *As if I heard*
a bell ring (as on a game show? Did I give
the right answer? Did you feel an echo vibrate
and change you? Did it go down to where
it hurts, there where you *really* live,
deep, deep, stay there and resonate;
did I send your drowning parts some air,
some comfort?).

        What I'm trying to say's
after the dream comes the specific place
you lie dreaming — the garden, or the fall from grace.

The Idea Of Love Between Us

It was a vision he had, a candle he lit,
something he cupped his hand around and held
gently, then gave to me: *"Here, you hold it
a while"*; and it flickered, and was frail, and smelled
wonderful. But it was like having a child
with no pregnancy, no time to prepare,
no clothes or ready bed, no room built,
no house. Where to put the child? Where?
No, it wasn't a child, it was a lit
vision. *"Here, you hold it,"* he said, and split.

Dear Julia,

There were clues,
    but I ignored them.
There were heavy dues,
    but I went toward them

with my pockets turned out
    and my palms twitching
and my smile;
    and love was an itching

that wouldn't stop,
    a voice
to be heard, a crop
    to harvest, a bird

to sing each morning —
    love! Like a Sousa
band — without warning —
    a flood let loose.

Shit. There were traces,
    but I went on,
thinking, *well, in these cases...*
    but there's no foregone

conclusion. No books
    can say, and no therapist
could point me away
    from love; *insist-*

ing. Insistent.
    As you who know
me know, persistent,
    and not inclined to go.

Hints are only hints
    until the evidence
is in. Innocence
    is assumed. Chances

are to be taken.
    And besides,
I was not the only
    one with clues, and guides

saying, Watch your step!
    There's a bus behind
this truck, and demons
    in that mind.

Love was a
    crowded highway to cross
on foot, because a
    keen sense of loss

wouldn't let me stay put.
    What? Why did I decide
to cross that road?
    To get to the *other* side.

Let's just say,
    it's not what I hoped
for, came all this way
    for. There's a hideous downslope.

All those clues. Hey,
    but I loved him very much.
That's my news—
    stay in touch—K.

The New Friend

The Tender Gesture Can Resurrect The World

The tender gesture can resurrect the world
that's fallen out around you, heedlessly, again.
It needn't be much: a finger lifting your chin,
and lips touching your eyes, cheek on herle
of hair — oh to let out the cry, a skirled
longing that may be as old as the begin-
ning of you, when you screamed, *Outside, let me in*!
and were human, alert, and uncurled
and probably already terribly hurt.
I've had the wish to dissolve myself
when it was too much, in a whisper, a stealth
of undoing; to con-, or sub-, or retrovert.
The gesture of despair projects
louder than words; tenderness surrounds and resurrects.

Care

is a painting you return to every day;
to add another stroke, to follow another line;
to make it real by the way
you consider; to make me yours, to make you mine.
...is a sculpture peeled from the nothingness,
marble, clay; here a fingerprint, here a swirl.
Here — (I need your eyes to look at this)
a question mark; what *is* it now? A girl?
A dream, a weight? A body watched and pressed
into life? *You* watch and press, breathe
me back — sometimes barely touched, sometimes caressed.
Carefully circling, you gradually unsheathe
(it, her, me). For all this labor, love, in the end,
will be the prize; love of an art, love of a friend.

Care II

I've sent you a poem; your first glimpse
of how, in that other world, I speak.
It is a lifeline thrown to you, since
things have changed between us. Though I feel weak
wondering how *you* will be struck by this,
I'm strong with the sense of this new thing, this freak
version of me; because the poem, "Care," is
one that came in a kind of trance —
which means I don't know where it came from, or how
it moved itself from thought to thought, sequenced
without help of logic. All I did was allow
it. Yet it says what I want
to say to you: love's a specter which haunts
the living back to life. You see, the peak
of it is not in the couplet ending,
the rhyme, the period; but in the sending.

...You know how it is when you're a child:
you *hear* your body move; you hear
the blood rushing in your ears, and your wild
heartbeat on the mattress. Strong and clear,
the blinking of your eyes; and when you close
them, ecstatic colors surge and press
against the lids, like the heart that's racing in your breast.
The colors—yellow, grass-green, rose,
turquoise—explode in rhythmic bursts; and the dark
is never dark. And the sleeping
body's never still. The docked barque
is always rocking; gazelle-heart leaping,
heaping jewels in the eyes, and feeding dreams
to every cell. Perhaps it is the sound of growing;
future You's teasing at the undertowing,
and firebirds bursting at your seams.

First Response—An Aubade

First response—to birds singing: it's the same way joy
always looks—eyes alerted, smile; there's the same boy
who raised his bar mitzvah champagne to the skies—
There he is! Same teeth, same eyes—
Tackle him! Pull him on you on the bed and say,
I have never loved anyone the way
I love you. First response to the first glimpse
of him waking to the morning birds: palimp-
sest on other mornings, other loves; for we are at once
  haunted
and free—there's only us—and yet there's *they*, who once
  we wanted...
At the first reaching of the new day's arms: heaven
rises from my feet where cat-like it reposed—seven
A.M.—to meet my brain which takes a rapid scan
and re-cognizes—oh! you! you!—as if we'll never have
to leave—for now, no grief, no disarray; just the clean stave
for the music of the day—notes of birds—legs—legs and lips
(oh god I love it so when we take trips).
The boy's the man; the girl's the woman, all rolled
in one—what kind of day? a *kind* day, sunny, cold—
and he's *already* being funny—I thank the gods I can still
  fall—
in winter—fall; and hold as if to hold—it *is*—is all.

Five Urban Love Songs
I. Central Park

Can one think, in sunglasses, in the park; think
with the children playing and the adult banter,
and someone smoking; and experiment, in ink,
through the invading dogs, and toddler-gallivanter?
Escape the *Ice-cold-beer-and-Snapple* hawking
and the ones who target you when you're alone,
and so they stare, or come over, talking?
But how can I (who've been rather accident-prone)
forget it was just that dappled fate-and-chance —
and perhaps the shade of arrogance —
that brought me *you*? and though I tried to shake
you off ("Don't bother me; I'm *mean*, I'm *grieving*")
the discouragement didn't seem to *take* —
so I came to accept that you weren't leaving.
Then I'll let these clowns distract me with their dance —
there's a weird wisdom in persistence —
I'll stick to my mount of grass and moss and clover,
writing things down, and thinking things over.

II. San Francisco

Pierced tongue. Do-it-yourself lisp.
What is this? Penitence? Native wisdom?
Mutilation? or signal: *I'll do anything*.
Was it a dare? or a careful plan? Did it sting —
or ache — and does the food get caught —
and should such a person *work* in a restaurant?
Customers' stomachs can turn — or does desire
turn to *her* — to wish — to feel the fire
glide over the silver (or is it gold?) pin?
And you, my darling, with your end-
less speculation: *Is he — is she — gay?*
Does he or she want you — or me — or either way?
Why do you need to know? I am *here*.
This is my body; eat. Unwrap. Disappear.

III. Portrait Of David As/Not As A Refrigerator Magnet: Universal

appeal; the most beautiful stone to pull
the image from: *David*. David of the tilted head,
the hip slung into, the arm I lived to till
the underbelly of. On my pillow, on my bed,
your body, David, undressed and dressed...
Now who's this in *plastic* plastered against
the refrigerator door! Not David! on whom they've pressed
pants, t-shirt, shoes; now the penis can be fenced
in skivvies; heaven-on-earth, figleaf,
in sunglasses! What they have done or think
they've done—appropriation; in short, in brief:
anyone's. Possessed, asked, *Shall we have a drink
now or later? Your place or mine?*
to toast the front—to dream the spine...

IV. Safe-T-Man

"This unique security product looks incredibly real, with moveable latex head and hands, and air-brushed facial highlights."   *advertisement*

If safety can be had from hollow men
whom one can place to fill the empty chair,
let's leave them to their task of sitting, then,
while I'll these blow-up men to you compare:
    Far off you pose, endangered, rare —
    and, coated as you are with scent and skin,
    you are surely filled with hotter air;
    still, neither heart can quite admit me in.
    Though Safe-T-Man can dress for many roles —
    wearing hats for winter or for tropic breezes —
    in commuter lanes, the *real* men can count tolls;
    yet...do not fold to fit precisely in valises.
To buy or not to buy the button-on legs — ?
Can anyone be safe? the question begs.

V. Help Me — A Flashback

I turned to you as if to say: *Push him out!*
Touch me with your brave new hands; erase
him from my ribs, from my arms, from my face.
Let your lips be rain falling on the drought
in my body —

          Then I was reaching
(as if I *could*) and perhaps you were fooled
into thinking me ready to be pulled
away. You wanted me, and I was beseeching
you — *Then help me* (for I could make no better
offer — it was a start — than a promise to try)
push him out! But he pushed back and I would cry
and you would kiss and as my eyes grew wetter,
you would *know*; and become angry and empty and cold.
What could I tell you — but what was already told?

At Sea

The Latest

news breaking: the hurricane crashed and burned.
Sad over kiwi sorbets, we fax and telex
to our shores; then later, forego food and sex
because here at sea the tables have overturned.
Wave-drugged, I fall asleep towel-wrapped on decks
that scoop and toss and rise and dip and surge;
this variation-on-a-rainy-day, the sea spray specks
erase habit from my skin, and this sick being merges
with the child home from school that I always
can become... By the time we get (for *some*one's
well enough to drive!) to be Phoenixes raised
groggily from berths, the guiding sun's
set and the heavens headline their own stars:
We're In Charge! So Go Back to Your Bars.

Lines Written While Reading Keats'
Isabella; or, the Pot of Basil

I

The murderous spite of pride and avarice, the dark
  Pine roof in the forest, weak bleat of love
In a heart that can barely sputter and spark
  Its host-body on — so (in that black grove)
Have we left hero and heroine, and mark
  Our place — lamplight in a shadowed cove —
By turning a triangle in the page-
Corner, then look back to life, our pilgrimage.

II

Have tides turned, with time? There are brothers,
  Still, who storm their sisters' dreams and leave
Them dazed and crumpled and without their other's
  Gaze, to hold that face inside and grieve;
Who've done the dirty work for merchant-fathers;
  Who've never slipped a finger up a sleeve,
Never brushed their lips across a cheek,
And never heard a beloved speak.

III

Those who have heard their loves cry out in need,
  And let them know that they will always come,
Cannot bear to watch deception and misdeed
  Guide the vile to their vain palladium —
Not caring who falls starving as they feed,

Or who they slash and stab, ad libitum.
(But do they not, inside some lonely hour,
Fall to their knees, weeping, empty, sour?)

IV

For love that leads away from wintry cold
   (As earnestly was pressed on me to feel);
For love that keeps us young when we are old;
   That leads a soul retracted to unsteel
(And you must taste the blossoms that unfold,
   Sharp as chives, soft as chamomile);
For the general award of love we live
And watch and wait and suffer and forgive.

V

Humanity that wars and maims and plots
   To maim and war has nothing made by death-
Time but a garden that forever rots.
   Why plant anything in such an earth?
Who waters with her tears her basil-pots,
   Though lost, at least has loved while drawing breath.
Better to die once-loved—although betrayed—
Than live untouched and bitter and afraid.

Two Millionaires, Isadora Duncan, And You

Of course he took the largest suite on the boat,
And we had a special menu printed every night!
Travelling with a millionaire really does simplify things,
And we had a magnificent time, everyone bowing left and right.

The American tour was happy, successful, and prosperous —
For money attracts money — until one day in January
A very nervous lady came into my loge and exclaimed,
"But my dear Miss Duncan, it's visible to everybody

From the front row! You can't continue like this!" "My dutiful
Mrs. X," I said, "that's what I mean my dancing to express —
Love — woman — formation — spirituality — the fruitful
Earth — the Madonna — that's what my dancing is!" But my bless-

ed state was really becoming quite visible. So we stopped
The tour and returned to Europe. "My love," L. asked,
"How would you like to travel up the Nile all winter?"
And excepting that master, Neurasthenia, we basked;

But like a black hand covering the sun, it appeared from time
*To time...*Elliot had tons of money, and knew
how to spend it; he occupied the penthouse cabin with its two
    jacuzzis
(indoor and out), the private balcony, spectacular view —

But Parkinson's disease gave him constant listing,
weaving motion, fluttering wrists, lips
opening more often than he spoke. He did his jittery
dance, bringing him up too close too often, hips

brushing yours inadvertently. He had come aboard
with his wife, and installed his mistress
in the only other penthouse, smoked a bit of weed
each day to erase the pain's progress...

Money isn't everything. How they came and went—
characters in a Mozart opera; except the hero couldn't do
    dances
as well as he once did, and his voice dispelled
in a stutter. Still, the elements, the comedic entrances

and exits in quick succession, people hidden in closets and
on balconies—you see what I mean? (As for me, I
look for you, my friend, in all the parks I walk in, hand-
some man; and do not want to—no I do not—say goodbye.)

What do I remember of that trip to Egypt? The purple
Sunrise, the scarlet sunset, the wind moving sand in waves;
The camels; laborers drawing water on the shore, moving frescoes
Where labor can be beautiful, even for the slaves...

George Sand (1839)

I. Empty Space

Empty space and still life freeze me with dread,
and symmetry and meticulousness fill me with gloom;
and if I try to imagine eternal damnation, my Hell
would be to live forever in a room

that is sparsely furnished and austerely tidy,
(unless it is occupied as a kind of tent);
for only one who is empty-headed and cold-hearted
could live without the living complement

of knick-knacks and bits and pieces, all signs of life —
a bird in a cage, or a vase of carnations —
where order rules supreme, nothing is worn out
or broken, and nowhere the perfume of sensations.

Perish all carpets in the world if I can have one
only on condition a child or cat will never play on it!
I cannot enter such a house without anger
and despair —

and that is all I'll say on it.

II. The Pig Ship

I have visited the island of Majorca thanks to the pig;
for, ever since three years ago permission was accorded
for their exportation via a small and beautiful rig
purchased in England, once a week to Barcelona
two hundred pigs — with a few passengers alongside — are
  transported.

It is quite touching to see the tenderness and care
with which these gentlemen (and I do not mean
the passengers) are treated. The captain has acquired,
by long association, a little of their impudent air
and a grunt in his voice rather like their own.

If a passenger complains of the noise they are making,
he replies it is the sound of waves of gold coins breaking.
If some lady complains of the foul odor which permeates
the ship, he tells her it is money's scent re-entering the gates.
And a seasick passenger's complaints are merely lost
among the needs of the pigs, who, when they are ill,
exhibit a tendency to surrender the will
to live, which must be combated at all cost.

Needless to say,
once we made port, we longed to get away
from such strange society; but leave was not granted
for us to step into the light of day
till every last pig was landed.

III. Travel

Why do you travel, my dear friend, why do you do it?
"I travel in order to travel." What is this need,
this costly, tiring, and sometimes dangerous pleasure,
often disappointing, to which we give way, on which we feed?

All of us, as soon as we have an opportunity,
travel; for the importance is not in
so much the travel, as in the getting away. Who among us
hasn't some yoke to cast off or grief best forgotten?

I imagine the human race as living two sets
of lives, one characterized by studious meditation,
domestic bliss, philosophic contemplation;
the other involving, above all, ideas and artistic inspiration.

Travel combines duty (congenial interchange, fresh
contacts) with pleasure—but the majority
of us travel in search of mystery, isolation, spurred
on by resentment of easygoing, "normal" society.

I set out to satisfy a desire for quiet and rest,
some remote noiseless retreat, where a day would have
twelve hours, there would be no need to remove my dressing gown,
and I would never be an unwanted visitor's slave.

Who among us has not at some time dreamed
of forsaking his affairs, his habits, and even his friends
to go live without cares, responsibilities, and above all,
without newspapers, on some deserted island?

But when we flee from the bustle in search of peace
and oblivion among people who weave life's thread
more slowly, we experience unforeseen troubles and regret leaving
the present for the past, the living for the dead.

This quite simply is what the theme of my narrative will be.
"Though one of us was dangerously ill, we undertook to cross
    the sea..."

Another Urban Love Song:
Souvenir de Florence...David Continues On His Way

David, outside the *Accademia*, makes an appearance
on t-shirts, alongside Adam touching God
's hand. Down the block the pilgrims plod,
viewers of all ages, adherents
to all faiths, come to worship or to gape:
"He's got a big one," a schoolgirl cries
in the interior, sunlit, space;
nearby, the Slaves' unfinished eyes...
Outside again, David "hung" on a postcard, sun-
glasses on the shaft: "Hi from Florence"
(it says) — *Wish you were here, love you, hon.*
Fascination and abhorrence —
yet I cannot resist reporting. (If we ever break up,
love, I want the Stonehenge coffee cup...)

The Death Of Albrecht: A Trip To See *Giselle* In Odessa

"The best thing in the letter is your address on the enve-
lope, which I had forgotten, and the worst is the death of
Albrecht."   Chopin, *letter*

I.

The Odessa Ballet has been engaged for *our* benefit,
tourists pouring off the ship at twenty-two
dollars a head; excepting for us, the crew —
a steal at twelve. Actually I got wind of it
that these "command performances" are all this ballet
troupe can give: musicians, danseuses, premiere and assoluta,
to be paid five dollars each to *assembler*
on a few evenings' notice. (No season, no future
engagements. Have they a class? a school? a master
to oversee them?) Still, they start to show up — they tune;
a violinist here, a bass, an oboist testing the faster
passages; while backstage, I presume, the Wilis — ah, bassoon! —
will make a troupe. Is it yet an orchestra? Pour champagne
("*Two dollar a glass*") at Intervals, so no one will complain.

39

II. Rules Of The Game

Rule Number One: Never Show
Your Wealth, When Courting A Peasant Gal. She'll
bolt. Or blush, curtsey, kiss your hand, then go.
That's when some...*gamekeeper* will come and steal
her from you. Hide yourself. Your creed:
bravery, modesty. Staying just this side of shabby.

Rule Number Two: Never Show Need
When At Your Poorest. Don't be grabby
among the rich, even when you're starving.
Let them admire the velvet curtain, the mended
costume, and all the *tours jeté* you're carving.
(Weep only when the curtain has descended.)
You might seem to be noblemen in peasant dress.
One must always try to hide one's wretchedness.

III.

What remains (story, style?) when precision
's had to give? Or is this some fragment
of the company, some subdivision
left while the others tour, heal, or defect?
Still, she is, and should be, a celebrated
character study, from simple happy peasant
to haunting apparition, willowy, shaded.
How the world turns. The lovely Unpleasants
come out from their limbo to snatch
their victim, love-torn, hallucinating, true.
(Isn't the Romantic Era a bitch?
All those handkerchiefs and billets-doux.)
Ah Albrecht, don't go there searching, please, don't go!
Graveyards can be dangerous places, don't you know?

IV. Intermission

Truly, it is among the most beautiful theaters of the world,
ivory-coated, be-statued; royal maroon sweeps
over the staircases, the marbled majesty-swirled-
in-majesty. I pocket a tiny prize off the floor, a keep-
sake, the smallest nesting doll of a set sold
at officially high dollar prices. Everywhere the enterprising!
Now to search for the hallway rest rooms; we're told
to follow the balcony's curve. What we find—not surprising—
does not measure up; or perhaps it is the counterpart
to all the fancy rest: holes in the floor. And a chain to pull.
No door locks. (To drink champagne was not so smart.)
What can one do? A "small container," when it's full,
must be emptied. Oh, well. We take
our seats; at least it's *Giselle*, and not *Swan Lake*.

V.

For many of our crew, I'd guess, it was their very first
ballet. Afterwards, some praised the loopy leaping
and the dramatic death of Albrecht (who was the *worst*).
But others simply missed it; they were sleeping.
We musicians did not love the orchestra
much; the violins each in their own country; the oboe
about a half-step sharp, the enthusiastic ta-ra
of the trumpets, the tympani who tried to steal the show.
But more, the Whole Thing made for alarm
over the great Russian Ballet's reputation.
I know, Odessa's the Ukraine, a separate *port de*...arm;
a liberated *bras*—a separate rumination.
Albrecht, spraying repeatedly across the stage,
re-enacting the death of an...death of an...age?

VI. The Wilis

It was when they "danced him down" that I got restless,
his exhaustion a sort of rise-slide-
collapse, rise-slide-collapse. Oh breastless
beasts! Why did he fall on the same side
always? This could have been the most realistic
part! (I felt the same about *Le Sacre*.)
I'd like to see them *really* go ballistic.
Exhaustion lives in dancers' every chakra,
alongside the Delirious Joy which is their due.
Are they afraid that it would ring too true?

Later that night, or the next, we sit
in the lounge-cum-bar which is our concert hall
every third night or so, discussing it.
(Those who did not go are reassured
they did not miss the performance to end all
performances, rather something to be endured.)
In a fit of inspiration, I fling
myself to the floor in imitation
of our Albrecht. The captain, who was sitting
(unseen by me) a half-room down,
sends drinks for all. Another kind of transfiguration.
Why be tragic, when you can be a clown?
The lounge singer blasts us with her song.
Oh, I don't know. We all get off; the ship sails on.

Diary Three

Last night after supper with D. and B., a real game of whist.
But I am ill and do not see the end of my sickness.
Awoke today with a pain in my throat and nausea, even so
 I worked.
Sasha, Nata, Cousin. Picked lillies of the valley with Bob.
Had a pain in my heart which frightened me. Nonetheless,
 a morning walk.
Very dissatisfied with the ideas that come to me, angry

because of bad luck. Am I played out? Wrote to N., was angry
on returning home because lunch was not ready. Whist
foursome after supper. A miracle—I won! Magnificent
 day—walked
all morning in the Trostyanka Forest—walked long and
 didn't feel sick.
Took part in the *pas de géant* after tea with G., B., and Bob.
How hard it has become for me to work!

I strain myself too much in my work.
Was again furious, malicious, and angry.
Did not mention tonight's strange dreams, rambling with Bob,
the Tarnovsky governess, etc. English language, whist
after supper. Played the piano long, returned home half-sick.
Looked at a wonderful sunset. Drank tea, walked

45

in the garden. The day was so-so. In the morning took a
   short walk
on the road to the railroad station. Worked.
This whist threesome irritates me so that I make myself sick!
Nothing results — except for being upset and angered.
Then to what purposes do I play whist? *Whist*
with E., duets with my darling, the incomparable, ideal Bob.

Ah, how perfect is Bob! How fascinating is Bob!
How perfectly charming he is in his white suit. Walked
to the railroad station. Flegont is ill, so played whist
with Lev (very dull) and for long, as I am ahead in my work.
Because Sasha set me two tricks in hearts, I got angry
as a madman. Oh, Peter Ilyich! Shame, Holy Father! *I've*
   been sick

since morning. So exasperated, I imagined I would do harm. Sick
at the thought of going away. I think it's on account of Bob.
Finished the andante, with which I am very satisfied. Less angry
than usual. Played some of my songs for Bob. Before dinner,
   walked
to the forest and back. God, how I love him! Managed to work
just a little. *There was no whist at all. I confess, whist*

is almost a necessity for me. Walked all morning. Sick
all day, though I worked well. *Nata, cousin, Bob*
(on horseback). Then whist and endless anger.

46

Want And Love

Martha

After Martha Graham

Where can she turn to find her answer?
There as it seems the gods propel —
Where you must move in measure, like a dancer.

She feels it, knows it is her chance for
life. She reads her bones — they spell:
There you can turn to find your answer.

The contraction that, in fact, expands her
becomes her cornerstone — drama unparalleled.
You must move in measure, be a dancer.

Stare in mirrors, catoptromancer.
The men you love you will repel.
They'll not turn out to be the answer.

It grows inside her, the entrancer
that will never be expelled —
Do not dance like any other dancer.

Your letters to the world — in glance or
gesture, breath and fall — will be upheld.
Who could she turn to — *There was no answer*
but to move in measure, like a dancer.

Erick And Martha

When he came—in contrast to her small
troupe of women-followers—into her rooms, her life,
there was a kind of hush overall,

underlain with rumors. The Crackers, as they were called,
had thought men were forbidden, *treif*.
Then in he came, a contrast to her small

figure—though she had never *seemed* small,
never meek. She began to fear, to need to be safe,
or saved. There was a kind of hush over all

complaints, except her screaming, biting—the call
of a wild one being tamed, fighting for her life.
When he came into her small,

ordered studio, he shrank the rooms and walls;
stepped on toes; and, finally, made a wife
of her. There was a kind of hush, over all;

but would it last? The wise, before the fall,
said, *There will be an end to all this strife,*
and he will go out—this fire, by contrast, small.
And there will be a hush, again, over all.

Want And Love

But why is desire suffering?
Because want leaves a world in tatters?
How else but in tatters should a world be?
    Molly Peacock, *Why I Am Not A Buddhist*

Want did leave a world in tatters.
Want, and love. (*Did I say wanton love?*
Oh no.) This is what I was thinking of —
that the former is Need Imagined, and the latter's
Need Known. Imagined Need can never
be met; but Love, real love, can be held out —
given not to be taken back, ever,
ever. Which is the turning of doubt
back at the gate; saying, *Do not enter*
this house. Do not enter this Being;
which is the gift that comes from center;
which is the sight that comes from seeing.
Let brave walking Love shine on Need behind.
Love has a vision. It's Want that's blind.

And Then There Is That Incredible Moment,

when you realize what you're reading,
what's being revealed to you, how it is not
what you expected, what you thought
you were reading, where you thought you were heading.
Then there is that incredible knowing
that surges up in you, speeding
your heart; and you swear you will keep on reading,
keep on writing until you find another not going
where you thought — and until *you* have taken
someone on that ride, so that *they* take in
their breath, so that *they* let out their
sigh, so that they will swear
they will not rest until they too
have taken someone the way they were taken by you.

for Agha Shahid Ali

Sometimes, Consciousness

Sometimes, consciousness is an ether that floats
in a jar you must keep a lid on; see how the vapors
hug the edges and cure the glass. Sometimes it's notes
that can be heard peeling across the neighbors'
lawns. Sometimes it's chattering like horses' hooves—
nothing you can decipher, but you know it's *going*.
You see, it's essence; it moves as spirit moves
you; as if you're leaves a wind is blowing.
Sometimes, then, *thought's* what you want to hold,
and so you try, but you must be as ether quick
and sly. It can be, to touch, so very cold—
or warm as love; but try to make it stick
and you cannot, you cannot except
by letting it—a balloon—go; trust someone else to intercept.

How Sonnets Are Like Bungee Jumping

It's the calculated danger—leap! The form will hold
you—will be as arms around you—ropes—
so when you say: *If I could be so bold…*
it says, *Okay, then, go! Spew out in hopes!*
There's safety in measure—like a mother
back at the shore, singing: *Swim out, and wave!*
Or (my Alexander teacher would say) a big brother
in your spine: *He's here; be brave.*
What's scary for someone's nothing for
another; to say, *Love*; to say, *I love,*
may be frightening as all get-out. And for
the very lucky, a poem can be a glove
that fits the hand that is your soul.
Oh, we jump in pieces; and some of us land whole.

Daybook

"It is necessary to study the words you have written, for
the words have a longer history than you have and say
more than you know."   George Oppen, *daybook*

Man on train: *You have to plan for success,*
but be prepared for failure; with all the assurance
of his squint-eyed beefy-armed years. Compressed
in the next seat, splay-kneed, in cuffed brown pants—
an equally crumpled friend, throat guimped in tie...
What has happened to us humans here? and how? and why?
The wife awaits—is she glad, and does she kiss
the meaty face—and does she love the crooked
eye; and do the giant arms enfold—her weariness—
remembering how longingly they'd looked?
You who say that joy can no one flood or melt
for long, adamantly I will argue down;
flailing out as if I knew, as if I had already felt
twenty, thirty years of love growing, grown—
and writing words—write!—as if to show
a history I haven't had, of things I cannot know...

The Laws Of Falling Bodies

16th-century Florence: Into a meeting of the Florentine
Camerata, vigilantes for the preservation of monody,
burst young Galileo Galilei. "Papa," he said, "play
your *liuto* a moment; for I want to know if the speed of these
wooden balls, going down an incline, will increase
as they draw nearer the end of the slope.
See how I depend on your years of practice, hope
the rhythms you built into your *tocca*, strings, and brow
will support me in this launching of my theories now.
See, the incline that I built of mahogany and brass
markers—like even-spaced frets—will be the constant the
   balls pass
as they flow. Now you must turn your back to us,
so; then you can play without distraction, and let us
be your audience, watching, watching every fraction.
Play, Papa, play!"
                    And from Vincenzo's *passamezzo*
spilled forth the laws of falling bodies, *di Galileo*.

Erick

In memory of Erick Hawkins, (1909-1994)

Is there an afterlife, and does it have mirrors,
a studio with windows, wooden floors,
Noguchi light fixtures, a pair of yellow doors?
And are there dancers who'll dedicate years
to you, there? If we could take tours
of Heaven, would we see José Limon
down the street, and over, Hanya Holm;
on other corners, Martha Graham, Doris
Humphrey—still making dances, making mystery?
And room fulls of black-leotarded hopefuls; husbands
not calling, *Come home*; animosity banished
from brains, rivalry resolved, history
portrayed; arthritis cleansed from hands;
and would we find all our young-dead not vanished?
(We are still here...counting...counting on you
to look down, guide us; tell us what to do.)

West Side Y

Half an hour of stolen time. People have been
at you all day, a sort of: "everyone chow
down!", phonecalls and mail and naked men
at the Y, where you can't even go peacefully now
for a "stress-reducing swim"; leers, invitations
from—you say—all sides. Ignore, respond?

You flee.
      *Let me not be one of these humans
in pursuit of you.* (Did Narcissus jump *in* the pond
to escape another wink—though it was his
own?) No. No. I will not be one of those.
Talk to me, talk to me. Take this hand and press;
keeping—*absolutely* on—all your clothes.
If I've failed in all else I set out to do—
please, let me not chase you away…not *you.*

Bluebeard's Castle (At The Dakota Window)

> The head of Euripides or a tense
> Egyptian cat (so still, you feel
> it turns and stretches when you look away)
> are not more distant than a lover
> in a far country...
> > D. Levertov, *Solace, for N.P.*

Not only Istanbul feels far;
but Canada, New Jersey, Pennsylvanian hills.
You are far away because you simply are.

Even uptown feels far, and, standing on the fringe
of the park, spying you at the window,
you feel so far — but hope flies up! and then a twinge

of what I learned painstakingly (when the fist
I'd closed so tightly was peeled open, finger
by finger: that knot I'd made for those I missed):

That for every letting go, a splinter
of — something! — gathered inside my heart-
shaped fist, or fist-shaped heart, as a reminder.

So I am Bluebeard's castle! (Weeping
cell walls; bloodstained halls!) But I am not
Bluebeard, for there's no company I'm *keeping*.

Oh It Is All The Work Of Getting There

that wears you away, the urging,
badgering, pushing, pulling, anger surging
and retreating, the hungers and thirsts
and the eating, drinking, and bursts
of sweetness that come with promises to change,
the opening and closing faces, strange
turns of heart and tones of voice...
the pleading, and times when choice
is taken away and promised again—
it is the question inside the calm: *when
is the next storm?* It is touching a dream
of peace that lasts, and ease; and then the scream.
It is the hope that lifts
and drops you. And the taking-back of gifts.

Serenade

I've fallen asleep with your tears in my mouth.

They got there by a curving track
of lash and socket and cheek, fell south
and sidelong, trying to cycle back
to someone's source; this fluid we call
precious, as if the salt and water and the *soupçon*
of sadness make a magic potion. If I swallow
your tears will my own pain get gone?
Here, take some of mine inside of you.

Are we healing now? Or is it something that I dreamed?
This morning may be a nightmare coming true;
for nothing (as they say) is what it seemed.

Coda

First Poem For My Brother

I remember when you were so small you fit in
the drawer in the kitchen—second from the bottom—
not a big wide drawer but one of those secretive
narrow ones; I think we kept bags in it. It had a mobile
aluminum top to it that we slid back, and out
you popped, like toast, smiling; and I snapped
the picture.

           I remember when you were so big
it was hard to lift you, and so small
I brought you up the stairs where you
crashed forward like an imbalanced grocery
bag, and cut your lip. I carried you, crying,
to call the neighbors, thinking *oh boy I'm in trouble
now*; and over Mrs. L. came with three kinds of
antiseptic and two kinds of bandages. Now I call you
when my life has toppled over like a garbage bag
and my love, my impossible love has fled me as if I were
a swarm of bees and I say: *what do I do?* and you tell
me what you know.

           I remember when we controlled
the lives of cylindrical-bodied dolls who rode in cars
with round body-holes, Misters and Missus' with
hairless round heads, turning their heads in the cars
to look at each other; all one size in different colors;
and how my love's statuesque body towered
over me when he said, *I just want to be free.*
What can you tell me of freedom, I ask you,
and you tell me what you know.

Mostly

it is the kindness that I cannot bear,
that sets me off and sets me back. Mostly
it is the sweetwishes, the ghostly
kindness lingering in the air.
When I've pressed my sorrow down
onto a page, like a petal's pressed,
and have begun at last to digest
reality and a bit of food, the sound
of sympathy is what floods my chest
and bursts me. Then when I thought the worst
was over, comes another thirst
for you, sent by the sweetness guessed
by kind onlookers to be what I need.
When kindness kisses the wound, I bleed.

My Worst Nightmare

My worst nightmare was to be the couple
that arrived separately and pecked sideways
and then glided by each other, supple
as snakes. Those are the ones whose eyes glaze
over what's close by, and yearn for the prize
out there somewhere. I told you at the first
party we went to: *This is who I do not
want to be*. Maybe it's my fault. Maybe I cursed
us, jinxed us, put our angel on the spot.
That was the target I wanted to steer
clear of, my greatest fear; what did I do?
Maybe I drew our attention, so new, too near
a nightmare so accurate as to have been rehearsed.
How does one make a dream come true?
I had a dream. It was to be with you.

The Problem

The problem with your well-oiled mind
was how easily I slipped from it, along
with everything else...Or that there was a kind
of trapdoor; or a *revolving* door and a strong
wind; or, more precisely, a moat and tide.
Oh god! What a moat! When I sensed that last
large iron gate swinging upward;
when—from quite far off—I heard
that huge resounding *clang*—I ran back fast
to pound at the—but what was the use?
Broken fists, exhausted cries, tears of hope-
lessness—you refused, you still refuse—
(and you left no cracks, nowhere to grope)
to let anyone—not even me—inside.

After the Season

Do not talk to me just now; let me be.
We were up to our ears in pain and loss, and so
I am reuniting all the lovers, fishing the drowned from the sea.

I am removing daggers from breasts and re-
zipping. Making it clear who loves whom — please *go*.
Do not talk to me just now; let me be.

I'm redistributing flowers and potions and flutes, changing key;
rewriting letters, pulling spring out of the snow.
I am reuniting all the lovers, fishing the drowned from the sea.

I am making madness sane, setting prisoners free,
cooling the consumptive cheek, the fevered glow.
Do not talk to me just now; let me be.

Pinkerton and Butterfly make such a happy
couple; Violetta has five gardens now to show...
I am reuniting all the lovers, fishing the drowned from the sea.

The jester and his daughter have moved to a distant city.
Lucia colors her hair now, did you know?
Come, let us talk, sit together and be
lovers reunited, fished like the drowned from the sea.

Because

Because we love, this day, this age, more times than once;
because we enter our new love's rooms
with fear and wonder held out like candles; and in our guts'
casement all forms of grief and hope are stored perfumes,
which by sudden thoughts will be dispelled, unsealed;
because we want exactly what we do not want
(e.g., to be disturbed, unstopped, revealed);
because inside the timid wren's a cormorant;
because a heart will rise again from ash and effigy
knowing what it already knew but more;
logic and discouragement can't override its ecstasy
and so it goes after what it was looking for...
What strange perfumes will make a dream tonight—?
What candle ever burned so low and still gave light?

Notes

"The Tender Gesture Can Resurrect The World" takes its title from an essay by Erick Hawkins.

"The Laws Of Falling Bodies" refers to Galileo's incline, which can be viewed at the Museum of the History of Science in Florence.

"And Then There Is That Incredible Moment," is a favorite phrase of poet Agha Shahid Ali.

From "Five Urban Love Songs": "Portrait of David As/ Not As..." refers in part to the currently popular refrigerator magnet "David", which comes with a variety of clothes. "Safe-T-Man" is pictured in catalogs being stuffed into a carrying pouch. L.A. commuters notoriously prop him in passenger seats to qualify for car-pool lanes.

"Two Millionaires, Isadora Duncan, And You" paraphrases a story from Isadora Duncan's autobiography.

"George Sand" draws from Sand's book, *A Winter In Majorca* (translations by Ripon and Graves), in which she tells of her travels there with Chopin, though he is never referred to by name.

"Diary Three" is based on Tchaikovsky's diary.

Kate Light is a violinist in the New York City Opera and is involved in modern dance and theater. Her writing has appeared in *The Paris Review*, *The Christian Science Monitor*, *Western Humanities Review*, *Confrontation*, *Wisconsin Review*, *Hellas*, *Sparrow*, *Feminist Studies*, *Janus* and others. She attended the Interlochen Arts Academy and Eastman School of Music. Her association with the Erick Hawkins Dance Foundation originated in 1990, when she toured as a company musician and began training in the technique.